FAIRACRES PUBLICATIONS 238

FACES
IN THE
CROWD

Tony Dickinson

CONTENTS

Acknowledgements

This book is based on sermons and addresses given in an ecumenical setting at Christ Church, North Watford, and in the churches of St Peter, Chalvey; St Francis of Assisi, Terriers; and Holy Ghost, Genoa; to whose congregations they are dedicated with gratitude and great affection.

FACES
IN THE
CROWD

Introduction

Preachers and poets have made much of the fickleness of the crowds who form the backdrop to the story of Jesus's arrival in Jerusalem, and later to his arrest, interrogation by the Jewish and Roman authorities and execution. Perhaps the best-known example is Samuel Crossman's exquisite Passiontide hymn 'My song is Love unknown', whose third verse runs:

> Sometimes they strew his way,
> And his sweet praises sing;
> Resounding all the day
> Hosannas to their King.
> Then 'Crucify!'
> Is all their breath,
> And for his death
> They thirst and cry.[1]

But is this fickleness in fact a figment of these writers' imaginations rather than a reflection of the Gospel narratives and the realities of first-century Jerusalem? In the following chapters, drawing on insights from contemporary Biblical scholarship and from the history and archaeology of first-century Palestine, I attempt to explore events that took place in Jerusalem during the last week of Jesus's life, the composition of the various groups present in Jerusalem at Passover and the ways in which each of those groups interacts with Jesus and his band of followers. These are examined in roughly in the order in which they appear in the Gospels.

---

[1] NEH 86.

Interwoven with this analysis are three imagined reconstructions of encounters that might have taken place, and words that might have been said by three people who play a part in the Gospel narratives. Two of them are scriptural, one is entirely a figment of my imagination. These three individuals emerge from the crowds as a reminder that in the Synoptic Gospels, and even, to an extent, in the Fourth Gospel, there is a change of mood between the events leading up to Palm Sunday and the days that follow. Up to his entry into Jerusalem on Palm Sunday, Jesus has been in control: he has organized; he has taken decisions; he has acted. Suddenly all that has changed. From Palm Sunday onwards, with the single exception of the cleansing of the Temple, the Gospel record is the record of Jesus waiting, not of Jesus acting. It is no longer about a man who does things, it is about a man to whom things are done. As Matthew, Mark and Luke tell the story, Jesus is, or appears to be, a passive victim of the Jewish authorities, the Roman Governor, even Judas, his betrayer. He waits on their decisions. He has to. They are for him, quite literally, a matter of life and death. But what did those people think they were doing—the people who held the fate of Jesus in their hands? What factors influenced the arguments they put forward, the decisions they took?

In two interludes and an epilogue, I try to enter into the mind of Judas Iscariot, the Jewish authorities in Jerusalem, and Pontius Pilate. I have put into their mouths (albeit from a twenty-first-century perspective) words that they might have said and arguments that they might have put forward, as they pondered what to do about this disturbing figure, Jesus of Nazareth, so powerful in his very powerlessness—even in relation to those who claim to have the power of life and death over him.

The Crowds by the Roadside

On Palm Sunday, when the Passion Gospel is read at the Eucharist, church congregations often throw themselves enthusiastically into the role of the crowd baying for Jesus's blood outside the Governor's lodgings in Jerusalem. 'Away with this fellow!' they shout. 'Release Barabbas for us!' (Luke 23:18) And, when the governor shows signs of softening, 'Crucify, crucify him!' (Luke 23:21). In each of the Gospel accounts of the period from the entry of Jesus into Jerusalem to his arrest and death, the crowd is a significant presence in the drama—and sometimes, as in that dramatic scene at the Governor's headquarters, a principal actor.

But it is not necessarily helpful—or indeed true—to talk of 'the crowd' as if it were a single entity. The crowd which accompanies Jesus as he enters Jerusalem is almost certainly not the same as the crowd which threatens a riot on Pilate's doorstep a few days later, despite the generations of commentators, preachers and hymn-writers who have assumed, down the centuries, that they *are* identical and who have reflected on the fickleness of the mob. So perhaps it might have been more accurate to give this study a slightly different title, not so much 'Faces in the Crowd' as 'Faces in the Crowds'.

With that in mind, it might be helpful to begin by trying to distinguish who are 'the crowd', or 'the crowds', in Jerusalem at Passover. In doing so, we have to bear in mind that, in any place where large numbers of people come together, people will not always stay in the same group or groups, and that even those who *are* in the same group do not always share the same objective, or objectives.

In Rome, in 1994, a massive demonstration drew between two and three million people into the open space of the Circus Maximus and the surrounding area.[2] It had been called by Italy's trades unions in protest against new labour laws proposed by the Berlusconi government. But between the announcement and the event the man who drafted those laws was murdered by terrorists and the unions' demonstration turned into a national protest against violent terrorism of every kind. Many of those millions would have been in the Circus Maximus to protest against terrorism, but many would have been there with the demonstration's original purpose in view, that of firing a warning shot across their government's bow.

So, when we look at Jerusalem in the last week of Jesus's life, we see different groups with different agendas (pilgrims, residents, occupying forces)—all of them capable of taking to the streets or making their presence felt in other ways. There are the crowds on the street as Jesus entered the city. There are the crowds in the temple, 'listening to him with delight' (Mark 12:37), or 'astounded at his teaching' (Matt. 22:33); there are the crowds in the darkness, armed with swords and clubs; the crowds threatening to turn over the Governor's residence; the crowds who were there on Golgotha to witness the execution, the silent watchers, kept at a distance by Roman troops. As we look at each of those crowds, we can see something, at least, of their make-up and, perhaps, something of their mood and their motive, remembering that they will have come from a wide variety of backgrounds.

All of these groups could, and probably did, provide some of the faces in the crowds who surrounded Jesus during that last week. But each of these groups would have had very different attitudes toward him and in this chapter and those that follow

---

[2] An account of the demonstration is available at https://www.wsws.org/en/articles/2002/03/rome-m26.html (accessed 6 November 2025).

I shall look at them in some detail, beginning with the crowds with their branches, standing along the roadside.

Most of these will have been pilgrims. Pilgrims formed one of the largest groups making up the crowds which thronged Jerusalem at Passover time. They had come to Jerusalem for the festival, in the same way that Roman Catholics might visit Rome for Holy Week and Easter or devout Muslims travel to Mecca at the time of the *hajj*. Among them, some would be fairly local, arriving after a few days' journey from other parts of Palestine or Syria. Others would be visitors from further afield.

The latter would include not only the descendants of those exiled to Babylon or Egypt six centuries before, but also Jews from the communities which had spread across the Mediterranean since the time of Alexander the Great and his successors, establishing themselves in most of the major towns and cities in the eastern half of the Roman Empire, like St Paul's home town of Tarsus. In addition, there were visitors from many other parts of Europe and the Near East. Some of them are listed in Luke's account of the day of Pentecost in the Acts of the Apostles.[3] Others, we know from non-biblical sources, came from far away Germany and Gaul. Though they were less likely to be pilgrims.[4]

Many of the more local pilgrims will have come south from Galilee and would have been well disposed towards Jesus, knowing him as a wonder-working rabbi—or maybe something greater. Most scholars think that the Galilean contingent formed the majority of the crowd which cheered Jesus as he made his

---

[3] Acts 2:9–11.

[4] See the Roman historian Tacitus (*c.* AD 56–*c.* 120), *The Histories*, trans. Kenneth Wellesley (Penguin Classics, 1964) and *The Annals*, trans. Michael Grant (Penguin Classics, 1958) and the Roman-Jewish historian Flavius Josephus (*c.* AD 37–*c.* 100), *The Jewish War*, trans. G. A. Williamson (Penguin Classics, 1959).

entry into the city. Luke's account, and Matthew's, in their different ways, suggest this strongly. Matthew tells us that

> When he entered Jerusalem, the whole city was in turmoil, asking, 'Who is this?' The *crowds* were saying, 'This is the prophet Jesus from Nazareth in Galilee.' (Matt. 21:10–11)

The emphasis is mine. Luke describes the crowd as 'the whole multitude of the disciples' (19:37). John, writing later, tells us that it was 'the great crowd that had come to the festival' (12:12–13)—and who were already in Jerusalem—who came out of the city to meet him, so definitely pilgrims but probably not, in his view, Galileans.

But what about Mark? His account, the earliest of the four, offers the image of peasants cutting foliage from the fields as they cheer Jesus into the city with the cry of 'Hosanna', 'Save now!' (Mark 11:9–10), a royal acclamation in 2 Samuel 22:2–4 and 2 Kings 19:19, and a reference to Psalms 116 and 118, two of the Hallel psalms sung at the pilgrim feasts of Tabernacles and Passover. They seem quite hyped up, but were they expecting a Messiah? Their chant has a future, not a present reference. It is 'the coming kingdom of our ancestor David' (Mark 11:10) which excites them, not its present fulfilment.

However, as New Testament scholars since the eighteenth century have pointed out,[5] Jesus seems to set up some kind of expectation, with what one modern scholar has called his 'street theatre',[6] using the donkey, with its clear nod to Zechariah 9:9:

---

[5] Hermann Samuel Reimarus (1694–1768), *The Goal of Jesus and his Disciples*, trans. and introd. George Wesley Buchanan (Brill, 1970); Albert Schweitzer, *The Quest of the Historical Jesus: A Critical Study of its Progress from Reimarus to Wrede*, trans. W. Montgomery (A. and C. Black, 1910), 19.

[6] Ched Myers, *Binding the Strong Man: A Political Reading of Mark's Story of Jesus* (Orbis, 1988), 294.

Rejoice greatly, O daughter Zion!
   Shout aloud, O daughter Jerusalem!
Lo, your king comes to you;
   triumphant and victorious is he,
humble and riding on a donkey,
   on a colt, the foal of a donkey.

This is a reference to the messianic prophecies, but Jesus then immediately undercuts it by his action, or rather inaction, when he enters the city. After that theatrical entry he does not proclaim the coming kingdom, or anything like that. He simply goes to the temple, has a look round, and then, 'as it was already late' (Mark 11:11), returns to his lodging in Bethany, as any modern tourist might do. All very anticlimactic. But what happens after that brings him into conflict with another crowd, and we shall look at *them* later.

The Crowd in the Temple

When we look at Jerusalem in the last week of Jesus's life, we see different groups with different agendas, all of them capable of taking to the streets or making their presence felt in other ways. Now we turn to focus on the crowds in the temple, 'listening to him with delight', or 'astounded at his teaching'.

The Passover pilgrims, obviously, were additional to the 25,000 or so people who lived in Jerusalem at that time. Many of those residents were people whose living depended on the Temple and its worship.[7] At their head came the priests, the Levites, the temple police, those who were learned in the Law. They also included the traders who sold the birds and animals for sacrifice, those who changed money into the right currency for paying the temple tax, the various types of artisans who kept the building and its furnishings in repair, stonemasons, carpenters, carvers in wood and stone, workers in metal, those who made and repaired vestments, those who supplied incense and other spices used in worship, and those who baked the special 'bread of the presence'.[8]

---

[7] For most of the demographic and socio-economic information in this chapter I am hugely indebted to the classic study of Joachim Jeremias, *Jerusalem in the Time of Jesus: An Investigation into Economic and Social Conditions during the New Testament Period*, trans. F. H. and C. H. Cave (Fortress Press, 1969).

[8] Also known as 'showbread', this was a religious offering of twelve loaves of bread baked from fine flour and arranged in two piles of six loaves each and placed on a golden table in the Jewish Tabernacle and Temple.

On top of these specialized trades, there were the sort of workers who might be found in any city of the period, the first-century equivalent of 'the butcher, the baker, the candlestick maker'. Documents mention doctors, barbers, traders and merchants of various kinds, workers in cloth and leather, innkeepers, stable-boys, fullers, even road-sweepers. And, of course, there were the soldiers of the Roman garrison and the members of the Governor's staff—at least for part of the year—with their dependants, their administrative and secretarial staff and their household slaves.

Those whose livelihood and those whose power and status depended on the Temple, either directly or indirectly, would have been, at best, ambivalent about Jesus or, more probably, hostile—especially after he drove out the traders and the money-changers, an act which suggested a radical challenge to the status quo and the existing authorities. But that would not have been the view of many who *worshipped* in the Temple, the 'people of the land', the poor, the disabled people who survived by begging from worshippers and pilgrims. Any who felt themselves excluded or who resented the power and privilege of the high-priestly Sadducee families and the self-importance of the scribes and Pharisees, would have been among the crowds who 'listened to him with delight', and whose clear approval of Jesus's teaching held the authorities back from openly taking action against him.

The occupying forces (like the Jewish authorities) would have seen Jesus as a potential threat to public order, and therefore someone to be watched very carefully. Matthew, Mark and Luke all record how the main religious and political parties in the city—establishment, radical, or pro-Roman—tried in turn to lure Jesus into making a rash comment that could be used in evidence against him in a Roman court, or which could be spun against him among the people, and all failed.

The nationalists, too, the Zealots and their extremist sub-group the *Sicarii* (dagger-men), would have been interested in what Jesus said, but for very different reasons. They wanted a figurehead who could be used to raise the people against the Romans and drive the hated occupier into the sea. They were hard men who wanted a Messiah who could be used as a front. That is why the authorities were panic-stricken when they heard the children shouting in the temple, 'Hosanna to the Son of David' (Matt. 21:15), echoing the cries of the crowds as Jesus had entered the city. David was the emblem of an independent, militarily-strong Israel. David was the nationalists' hero — *not* a name to mention within the hearing of Rome!

The crowds who listened to Jesus in the Temple would have included members of all these groups: some praying for the kingdom, some waiting for the revolution, some looking for an opportunity to silence him. But because of the eager interest with which Jesus was heard by the crowds who regarded him as a prophet, it was not until one of the Twelve came forward with the offer to hand him over that the authorities could make any headway.

So, what was the teaching that made such an impact on the crowds? John tells us nothing, but Matthew, Mark and Luke offer their varied summaries of what Jesus said during those days in Jerusalem, agreeing that the crowds were spellbound (Matthew says 'astounded') by his words. They agree, too, that there were confrontations with the temple authorities after Jesus evicted those who were making money out of the pilgrims. 'By what authority are you doing these things?' they asked him. 'Who gave you this authority to do them?' (Mark 11:28, Matt. 21:23, Luke 20:21–2) Jesus answers them, as he so often does in such situations, with a question of his own. Here it is a question about the authority of John the Baptist — one which again points up the contrast between the religious leaders and the ordinary people, the people of the land, who saw John, and see Jesus, as a prophet—and Jesus follows it up, in all three Gospels, with the parable of the vineyard, a story which puts into question the legitimacy of the temple authorities.

At this point Matthew inserts the parable of the marriage feast,[9] again aimed at the Jerusalem establishment—and probably revised in the telling to take account of the horrific end to the Jewish Revolt of AD 66–70. Mark and Luke go straight into the various attempts, by the political and religious elite, the Jerusalem 'establishment', and a religious professional, to trap Jesus into making a statement which can be used against him and Matthew follows them, noting, after Jesus dismisses the Sadducees, that 'when the crowd heard it, they were astounded at his teaching' (Matt. 22:33).

These encounters with the Jerusalem authorities end with Jesus's question about the Messiah, which silences their hostile interrogation. 'No one was able to give him an answer, nor from that day did anyone dare to ask him any more questions.' (Matt. 22:46). At this point Jesus goes on the offensive with, in all three Gospels, some sharp public criticism of the scribes, given to the disciples, but 'in the hearing of all the people' (Mark 12:38–40, Luke 20:45–7). In Mark's Gospel, as in Luke's, these are short and to the point. In Matthew's account they become half a dozen full-blown 'woes', addressed to the Pharisees as well as to the scribes: for locking people out of the kingdom of heaven; for nit-picking interpretations of scripture and tradition; for a lack of personal integrity, play-acting the role of the upright and holy while remaining slaves to their own appetites; and ending with a spectacular denunciation of their complicity in shedding the blood of the righteous. It is a powerful indictment of religion gone to the bad in its desire to preserve the powerful and to exclude and oppress the powerless.

---

[9] Matt. 22:1–14.

No wonder 'all the people', so Luke tells us, 'would get up early in the morning to listen to him in the temple.' (Luke 21:38) And no wonder the temple authorities were plotting his death. Jesus was putting into words the peoples' sense of alienation from 'organized religion' and laying the blame for that alienation firmly at the door of the 'professionals'. It is a message which is as relevant today as it was two thousand years ago in Jerusalem.

First Interlude
Judas Iscariot

Jesus declared, 'Very truly, I tell you, one of you will betray me.' The disciples looked at one another, uncertain of whom he was speaking. One of his disciples—the one whom Jesus loved—was reclining next to him; Simon Peter therefore motioned to him to ask Jesus of whom he was speaking. So while reclining next to Jesus, he asked him, 'Lord, who is it?' Jesus answered, 'It is the one to whom I give this piece of bread when I have dipped it in the dish.' So when he had dipped the piece of bread, he gave it to Judas son of Simon Iscariot. After he received the piece of bread, Satan entered into him. Jesus said to him, 'Do quickly what you are going to do.' Now no one at the table knew why he said this to him. Some thought that, because Judas had the common purse, Jesus was telling him, 'Buy what we need for the festival'; or, that he should give something to the poor. So, after receiving the piece of bread, he immediately went out. And it was night. (John 13:21–30)

We begin our exploration of the motives of those individuals and groups whose decisions and actions made Jesus's death inevitable amid the warren of back-streets in the old city, not far from the Temple. Here, in a dwelling indistinguishable from any of those around it, a dozen or so men are sitting around a wooden table in an upstairs room, waiting. We have arrived in the middle of Thursday evening, round about the end of supper-time—and in fact there are empty plates and cups on the table. Outside in the street, someone is knocking on the door of the house. One of the group at the table signals to another, who goes out and down the stairs. We hear the street door open and a whispered

My brothers of the Resistance, fellow workers in the struggle for the liberation of Israel, tonight I bring you good news. Tonight I am able to report that we may confidently expect to throw off the yoke of Roman oppression from the necks of our people within a very short time, perhaps even before the end of this Passover festival.

Events have been set in motion which must inevitably lead to a great popular uprising in this city. We wait only for the signal to be given—and it will be given later tonight when I shall lead a detachment of the Temple police to arrest Jesus of Nazareth in a private estate on the lower slopes of the Mount of Olives. This arrest will, of course, be resisted by those of Jesus's followers who are with him, and the attempt may well fail. But I can assure you that, whatever the outcome, the fact that such an attempt has been made at all will be enough to spark off a blaze of popular protest in Jerusalem which the Roman governor and his troops will not be able to extinguish—not even with the support of the legions from Syria.

Those of you who were in the city earlier in the week will remember the great excitement and enthusiasm shown by the pilgrims when Jesus rode into Jerusalem. That demonstration may not have achieved all that some of us might have hoped, but it enabled us to test the waters. All of those pilgrims who cheered Jesus every step of the way into the city will still be here

until after the Passover Sabbath. With the help of our many sym-
pathizers we cannot fail to rouse them into a popular movement
fuelled by a great anger against the Romans. When once we have
put Jesus of Nazareth at the head of this movement, it will
spread more and more widely until it becomes a national uprising and the Roman oppressors will be driven into the sea.

The arrest of Jesus has been set up with the co-operation of
the Temple authorities. But they have their own agenda and they
know nothing of ours. As far as they are concerned, I am a dis-
affected disciple, who has become concerned at the radical
attitudes which Jesus has taken to the traditions of our fathers.
and increasingly disillusioned by his behaviour. They genuinely
desire to see Jesus out of the way. They rightly see him as hostile
to the way in which they have cozied up to the Romans in order
to preserve their own power against movements like ours which
speak for the great mass of people.

So it is possible that they will provide me with sufficient
force to effect an arrest despite the expected resistance from my
fellow disciples. Simon Peter, one of the inner circle from
Capernaum, and at least one other, will be carrying a weapon.
So I would suggest that you send someone to keep an eye on
how the situation develops and to report back. We can then
change our plans to cope with any contingency and, if anything
goes wrong, we can take appropriate counter-measures.

I am aware that a number of you are doubtful about the
wisdom of placing our reliance on Jesus of Nazareth as the figurehead for a movement against Rome. And I know that on
more than one occasion during the past year he has failed to give
the unambiguous lead for which we were hoping. He has given
tacit approval to contributions to the Resistance from his disciples' common fund. But he dodged our attempts last year to set
him at the head of a popular uprising in Galilee. Earlier this
week, he failed to give the complete endorsement that we might

have expected to the poll tax boycott, although equally, he did not give his support to those who argue that we must pay this unjust levy. And, of course, he did not make the fullest use of the opportunity which was provided by his entry into the city — it can only be described as triumphal — to rouse the people against the forces of Roman oppression.

But Jesus continues to be very popular with all sections of the people — except for those who have economic or political power: to them he is an object of the greatest suspicion. All those among the leaders of our people who have been contaminated by their association with Rome would love to see him safely out of the way. Now, it is true that he has himself had dealings with representatives of the army of occupation and with the governing classes, but these have been insignificant and purely humanitarian in their concern. The people involved have always been in subordinate positions — junior officers in the army of occupation, minor government officials in the customs and the revenue service. And don't forget that on more than one occasion Jesus has been instrumental in causing such people to leave government service in order to become his disciples. On the other hand, his attitude to those in high positions of authority has always been consistently and sharply critical, both in public and in private. Some of you have heard the sort of thing that he has been saying to the crowds. I have heard what he has said — even more sharply — to those closest to him.

Which brings me to my next point. Previous attempts to raise the mass of the people against Rome have usually failed because the leaders of the revolt have been identified with one particular class or region or sectional interest. Jesus of Nazareth draws support from all sections of the Jewish people both here in Judaea and in Galilee. He has some supporters in positions of very great influence, including one or two who are members of the High Council of the Sanhedrin, though I'm sorry to say that these people have not yet felt in a strong enough position to go public with their support. Jesus also has a tremendous moral authority, and our movement of national renewal is a moral and spiritual movement or it is nothing.

It cannot be in accordance with the will of God that his people are ground into the dirt by the heel of gentile oppression. Our Scriptures say as much over and over again. It is the sins of our leaders—the high-priestly clique, the Sadducees, Herod's supporters—it is their sins which have brought us to this state of subjection and demoralization. Jesus of Nazareth, on the other hand, has consistently proclaimed the coming of God's Kingdom of justice and freedom. This message is at one with our call for the renewal of our nation.

So we must somehow bring Jesus of Nazareth on board with us. Open attempts to persuade him or cajole him into supporting our cause have so far failed, but I am convinced that if he should be put in peril of his life by those who are his natural enemies just much as they are ours, he will finally be compelled to recognize that he and we are on the same side. And then he must inevitably lend his support to our uprising against Rome.

If his only alternative is death at the hands of his enemies and ours, I do not think that there can be much doubt about the choice that he will make. By staging his arrest in this way, we are offering him tonight the opportunity to be the great liberator of his people. I do not think that he is likely to refuse it.

THE JERUSALEM CROWD

When we look at Jerusalem in the last week of Jesus's life, we see large numbers of people gathered in the city, forming themselves into different groups with very different agendas. We began by looking at the crowds of pilgrims, mainly Galilean, who thronged the roadside as Jesus entered the city. So far we have threaded our way through the diverse crowds in the temple, skirting both those who were plotting the death of Jesus and those who were 'listening to him with delight' or 'astounded at his teaching'. Now, with Judas Iscariot, we come to the crowds in the darkness, armed with swords and clubs, and the crowds who, when morning broke next day, threatened to turn over the Roman Governor's residence.

As we have seen, those whose livelihood and those whose power and status depended on the Temple, either directly or indirectly, would have been either ambivalent about Jesus or, more probably, hostile—especially after he drove out the traders and the money-changers. We also recognized that the occupying forces would have seen Jesus as a potential threat to public order, and therefore someone to be watched.[10] We saw too that, because of the support which Jesus had among the ordinary people, the Jerusalem authorities had no opportunity to arrest him without serious risk of causing causing a riot and provoking Roman intervention at one of the most sensitive times of the year. John catches the mood well when he describes the Council's anxiety

---

[10] Gerd Theissen's book *The Shadow of the Galilean*, trans. John Bowden (Fortress Press, 1987) offers a fictionalized account of such surveillance.

that 'if we let him go on like this … the Romans will come and destroy both our holy place and our nation.' (John 11:48) It was only when one of the Twelve came forward to the chief priests, offering to hand Jesus over to them, that the authorities finally felt that they were free to take action.

And that is the point at which a very different crowd enters the story. The Jerusalem establishment takes its revenge on Jesus by sending out an armed posse 'with swords and clubs' (Mark 14:43 and parallels). The gospels differ as to who made up the posse. Matthew and Mark mention a crowd sent by the chief priests and the elders. Luke says that the chief priests, the temple police and the elders actually accompanied them. St John describes 'a detachment of soldiers together with police from the chief priests' (John 18:3) — language which suggests that it was a military or paramilitary force. If John's information is correct, the soldiers might possibly have come from the Governor's garrison, but they are perhaps more likely to have been part of King Herod's entourage. The police were the men who kept order in the temple. They turn up in Luke's account of Jesus's arrest, as well as in John's, and they appear again in the early chapters of the Acts of the Apostles.[11] They arrive at one of Jesus's regular meeting-places to arrest him by night, after the Passover meal (if we follow the timing of the first three Gospels), or on the evening before Passover (if we follow St John). Either way, it was a time when the great majority of those who might have supported Jesus are scattered and preoccupied with other things. There are no crowds here to be afraid of — only the disciples, and one of them has been 'turned'. Everyone else is on the payroll.

And this, presumably, is the core of the crowd who make it so difficult for Pilate to retain control of the situation when Jesus is brought before him early the next morning. Presumably,

---

[11] Acts 5:22ff.

too, the word would have gone around: to the people who made their living from the Temple, the people whose stalls had been trashed by Jesus, the people who had been stung by his criticism of their ostentatious piety and lack of concern for people who did not meet their high standards. This is not 'the crowd' that shouted 'Hosanna' outside the city, nor 'the crowd' who hung on Jesus's every word. This is 'rent-a-mob', as genuine an expression of popular feeling as the crowds of government employees in an autocratic state who are coerced into providing the backdrop for a speech by their leader. Many of them may have been people who would love to see Barabbas, the nationalist bandit, out of jail and Jesus out of the way. Barabbas might have been dangerous, but he was predictable. Mark tells us that he was 'in prison with the rebels who had committed murder during the insurrection' (Mark 15:7). As a nationalist hard man, he would have had his supporters and safe houses, but they would have been a known quantity, to the Jerusalem authorities if not to the Romans. Once Barabbas was released he could be traced and picked up again if need be. 'Crucify Jesus' looks a much more attractive option.

So the high-priestly families and their supporters get their man—at the cost of their integrity, and of their future survival. They play the Romans' game (John's Gospel spells out with great clarity why and how they play the Romans' game) and they bet their future on it. When Pilate asks, 'Shall I crucify your king?', they make a fateful decision. 'The chief priests answered, "We have no king but the emperor."' (John 19:15) And Pilate hands Jesus over to be crucified. In Matthew's Gospel the crowd's last word to Pilate is, 'His blood be on us and on our children!' (Matt. 27:25), a word that was fulfilled nearly forty years later when the high-priestly Sadducees finally lost control of Judaean politics to the heirs of Barabbas and Titus's vengeful legions stormed and flattened Jerusalem.

By now the sun is getting higher, and the news is spreading. Other crowds are gathering. The crowds who had listened, spell-bound, to Jesus when he preached in the Temple, the crowds who had followed their wonder-working rabbi all the way from Galilee, are out on the streets again—but it is too late for them to prevent judicial murder. They have nothing that can be opposed to the Romans' military power. Some of them turn to follow the procession to the place of execution. Some of them turn on Jesus. No one loves a loser—and besides, the Jerusalemites among them had to carry on living in the city. No point in making enemies unnecessarily. Others follow simply to see the end of hope and to mourn. We shall think about *them* in rather more detail shortly.

SECOND INTERLUDE
THE JEWISH AUTHORITIES

Now the festival of Unleavened Bread, which is called the Passover, was near. The chief priests and the scribes were looking for a way to put Jesus to death, for they were afraid of the people.

Then Satan entered into Judas called Iscariot, who was one of the Twelve; he went away and conferred with the chief priests and officers of the temple police about how he might betray him to them. They were greatly pleased and agreed to give him money. So he consented and began to look for an opportunity to betray him to them when no crowd was present.

(Luke 22:1–6)

We continue our exploration in the south-western corner of Jerusalem, in the courtyard of the house of Joseph Caiaphas, High Priest now for more than ten years. It is late at night—or rather, early in the morning— but the house is a blaze of light, and the courtyard is full of people. Many of them belong to the High Priestly household, or to one of the other great families of the Jerusalem aristocracy, or else they are attached to the Temple. Others are local residents from this quarter of the city, drawn by the hubbub, and by rumours about the events of the previous evening.

A door opens, and a figure emerges at the top of the steps leading down into the courtyard. He is recognised as a member of the Council, the highest authority in religious and Jewish civil matters in Jerusalem. The expectant crowd falls silent. The man begins to speak:

I have been instructed by the Court of the Sanhedrin, sitting in its capacity as the supreme court of justice of our people, under the presidency of High Priest Joseph Caiaphas, to explain to you the action which we have taken in the case of Jesus bar-Joseph of Nazareth, by whose claims some of you seem to have become convinced.

You will probably know by now that, acting on information received, our agents arrested him late last night during a secret rendezvous with some of his followers at a location just outside the city.

He is being held at present in the High Priest's house; later this morning he will be transferred, under guard, to the Governor's residence. There he will be tried under Roman law on charges of a political nature which have arisen from our preliminary investigations and from statements which Jesus bar-Joseph has made to the Council while under interrogation.

The action which we have taken so far has, I should add, the support of the overwhelming majority of the Council, and by that, I mean the overwhelming majority of both the main parties. The decision to arrest Jesus was not taken without serious consideration on the part of the authorities. Both lay and religious leaders have been fully consulted at all stages of this investigation, and they have given us, I am happy to say, their whole-hearted cooperation.

The initial reason for our interest in Jesus of Nazareth was the increasing anxiety that his teaching and activities have aroused among those who are concerned for the survival of our religious and cultural traditions — traditions for which, as I hardly need to remind you, our fathers, and their fathers, were not ashamed to lay down their lives.

It is doubtful whether a man like Jesus of Nazareth can appreciate the spirit which motivates such self-sacrifice. He has made it clear, during the three years since he first emerged as the leader of this new Galilean 'cult', that there is scarcely any aspect of our way of life which he regards as in any way sacred.

He has no time for the ties of natural affection. Family life in particular has been one of his main targets. It seems to be a condition of following him that men and women should abandon their families, often without any means of support. His treatment of his own widowed mother is, of course, notorious.

His attitude to our religion has been just as scandalous. His 'interpretation' of the Scriptures has been an affront to the piety of many devout Jews. In the writings of Moses and the prophets there are the clearest guidelines for living an upright and respectable life. Jesus of Nazareth's method of explaining away the clear teaching of Scripture has not only opened the doors of our synagogues to all sorts of undesirables, it has also caused some misguided people to lose all sense of right and wrong.

And we have, on many occasions during the past months, heard his wild attacks on the worship of this Temple. Many of you were witnesses of the disgraceful incident a few days ago when he physically assaulted those who provide the very necessary service of welcome for pilgrims to Jerusalem. Not only do these people help strangers to the city in overcoming currency problems and enable them to offer the correct sacrifices, they also make a small, but nonetheless vital, contribution to the upkeep of this magnificent building, whose sole purpose is to declare the glory of God.

These, of course, are primarily matters within our own jurisdiction. What has led the council to refer this case to the Governor is the unacceptable political implications of some of the teaching of Jesus of Nazareth. As you know, our leaders, and especially the High Priests, are continually involved in the most difficult and delicate negotiations with the occupying power. It is scarcely an exaggeration to say that the survival of our religious and cultural heritage depends on the success of these negotiations. Several of Jesus of Nazareth's sayings, not to mention his known association with members of extremist militant organizations, have made the task of negotiating with the Romans doubly difficult. I need hardly remind you of what might have happened if the ridiculous attempt at a triumphal entry into Jerusalem which his followers stage-managed last week had led to a confrontation between the crowd and the Roman garrison. Any encouragement of extreme political views can have only one outcome—the total destruction of our people and nation.

There is one final point, which I hesitate to mention because it emerged in the course of interrogation, and is therefore strictly speaking *sub judice* (if I may use the Roman expression) until after the hearing before the Governor. However, you ought, I think, to know that under examination before the High Priest, Jesus of Nazareth admitted what many of us have long suspected: namely that he believes himself to be above the Law, greater than Abraham our father, greater than Moses who gave us the Law, and indeed—and I shudder to say it—that he considers himself on a level with almighty God, the Holy One of Israel, blessed be He.

I do not need to emphasize the sheer appalling grossness of this blasphemy. It is for this reason that representatives of the Council will be pressing for the severest penalty—by which I mean nothing less than crucifixion—when we meet the Governor later this morning.

In the circumstances that I have outlined, the Council has authorized me to tell you how vital it is that you, and everyone else who is concerned to preserve our faith and our heritage—our very national identity, indeed—should be present to support our leaders at this meeting with the Roman authorities.

THE WOMEN IN THE CROWD

Returning to our reflection on the role of the crowd in the last week of Jesus's earthly life, we narrow the focus quite sharply to consider the women in the crowds.

On the whole, women do not figure prominently in the first part of the Passion story, which is, perhaps, not surprising when we remember that most of what happens after Jesus enters Jerusalem happens within the precincts of the temple. And women were excluded from almost the whole of that area. They were allowed further into the precincts than non-Jews, but not much further. The 'Court of the Women' was the outermost courtyard of the temple complex, inside the huge shopping mall and market-place which was the 'Court of the Gentiles'. The only woman who is noticed during those first few days in Jerusalem is the poor widow pictured by Mark and Luke dropping her tiny contribution into the temple's alms-chest and receiving praise from Jesus for the depth of her generosity.

Women, of course, play no part in the events of Maundy Thursday night. The arrest of Jesus is 'man's work'. On the other hand, we see a slave-girl (Matthew says two) play a significant part in the humiliation of Peter as he waits nervously in the courtyard of the high priest's house. And the governor's wife has a dramatic off-stage role with her message to her husband, 'Have nothing to do with that innocent man, for today I have suffered a great deal because of a dream about him' (Matt. 27:19), an intervention that has gained her canonization in parts of the Eastern Church, but which had no effect on the stand-off, except possibly to increase Pilate's discomfort. It would take a very strong character to decide a capital case on the strength of his wife's dreams—particularly when such a decision would probably send what was already a very tense political situation over the edge into a complete breakdown of civil order.

So, the men have their way. Jesus is condemned to death. And from this point women begin to have a higher profile. In his account of the march to the gallows, Luke tells us that 'a great crowd of the people followed him, and among them were women who were beating their breasts and wailing for him' (Luke 23:27). Perhaps they too had been among the crowds who 'listened to him with delight.'

But Jesus has no time for their sympathy. He warns them not to weep for him, but to save their tears for themselves, because disaster is coming on Jerusalem—so great a disaster that the childless will be counted happy, because they will not see their sons and daughters perish. Some scholars have understood his words in terms of the destruction of Jerusalem by the Romans. The late Bishop John V. Taylor, giving the Holy Week addresses to an ecumenical audience in Geneva nearly forty years ago, took them to be Jesus saying no to 'the easy spontaneous emotion, the quick release of tension': saying no, because such emotional release 'is misdirected and because it is dangerous.' This is not time to 'have a good cry'. It is time to weep for our sins, to weep for the love of the Son of God who dies, in the words of St Francis of Assisi, 'for love of our love'.[12] The warning of impending disaster is also a call to repentance, a demand from

---

[12] The 'Absorbeat Prayer', associated with St Francis but apparently older. The earliest citation is to be found in the anonymous tract *L'estat de la citez de Iherusalem*, 86, dated to 1180. Text in English and Latin at https://www.terrasanctamuseum.org/en/discover-more/historical-sources/ (accessed 6 Nov 2025).

the Cross that cannot be satisfied by a superficially emotional response. It requires a change of direction at the deepest level. John Taylor adds

> As we read the story again, incident by incident, we must be struck by the hard fact that two thousand years have not made much difference to humanity. The changes are only on the surface. When armed men get a victim into their hands, handcuffed and alone, they can't resist the urge to knock him about—he's fair game in the back room of Caiaphas's house or any other police barracks. Weep for yourselves. When someone who has learned to play the power game finds that his delicately balanced structure is threatened, it is still expedient to wipe out one unimportant but awkward individual to preserve that balance and keep the peace, whether the manipulator is the High Priest of Judaea or the President of where you will. Weep for yourselves. Those who have the power to insist that justice is done, still prefer to wash their hands of the matter, and crowds of ordinary, decent, frightened women and men yell the slogans of the moment rather than stopping to think and stand out against the rest. Weep for yourselves.[13]

He goes on to point out that it is not possible to regard the Cross of Christ from a vantage point of detached objectivity. The Cross draws us in. It involves us in what is going on. That was too much for all of the disciples except the one whom Jesus loved. The others were not ready to be involved. Nor were the daughters of Jerusalem. They offered their pity which, as Bishop Taylor notes, is one of the most deceptive of human emotions. He describes it as 'a halfway stopping-place on the way to discipleship'—and that is not enough. The disguised Viola in *Twelfth Night* offers her pity to the infatuated Olivia, who seizes on it as 'a degree to love', meaning closely related.[14] Yet, as Viola

---

[13] John V. Taylor, *Weep Not for Me: Meditations on the Cross and the Resurrection* (World Council of Churches, 1986), 2–3.

[14] William Shakespeare, *Twelfth Night*, Act III, Scene i.

points out, pity is often something that we show to enemies. Jesus does not seek our pity either for himself or for the brothers or sisters in whom we are meant to find him. He seeks, rather, the active love which feeds them and clothes them, visits them in sickness and in prison. He calls us to become involved in them at the level of both will and action

Perhaps, in this context, we need to reconsider the legend of Veronica. She was the daughter of Jerusalem who did not only lament over Jesus as he walked the way of the cross, she took off her head-cloth and applied it to his bruised and bleeding face. And, so the story goes, she was rewarded by a likeness of the Saviour's face imprinted miraculously on the cloth. The story, of course, is a medieval invention — or rather, the elaboration of an episode found in one of the apocryphal writings.

However, it has some interesting undercurrents. Scholars have long pointed out that the name 'Veronica' (which seems originally to have been applied to the cloth rather than the lady) can be interpreted as an anagram of two words, the Latin 'vera', meaning true, and the Greek 'icon', meaning an image. Veronica is, then, the 'true image' of Christ, not in the sense that some once claimed for the Turin Shroud, but in the sense that her act of kindness to a condemned man, her daring to get involved in the fate of a man rejected by the leaders of his people and handed over to death, is a true image of Christ's own concern for the helpless, the voiceless, the despised and marginalized. Her gesture of love and compassion holds the true image of Jesus.

But the grim procession moves on, and we move on, to the final act in the drama of Jesus's suffering and death. Cheap pity is out. So are the devout ladies who offer the condemned a cup of wine laced with pain-killer. Are they, I wonder, Mark's and Matthew's version of Luke's wailing women? We pass over the mockery of the passers-by, the satirical thrusts of the chief priests, the scribes and the elders, the abuse of the other condemned criminals, the hardened unconcern of the execution squad, and we come to three o'clock in the afternoon.

Jesus breathes his last. Matthew and Mark depict him as utterly abandoned — even, it seems, by God. His last words echo the Psalmist's cry of desolation, *'Eli, Eli, lema sabachthani?'* (Matt. 27:46, cf. Mark 15:34) The only people near him are the squaddies, dicing for his effects, and their officer.[15]

But beyond the military cordon, there are others. Luke says 'crowds had gathered there for this spectacle' (Luke 23:48) — a theme of 'witness' which he will pick up in the Acts of the Apostles.[16] Matthew and Mark agree with him that there were 'women … looking on from a distance', women who had come down with him from Galilee. Some of them are named, Mary of Magdala, Mary the mother of James and Joses, and Salome.[17]

These had been Jesus's support group when he was alive.[18] They are now the witnesses of his death and burial. Some of them will go to his tomb after the Sabbath to pay the final tribute of friendship by anointing his corpse.[19] John locates some of them, with the mother of Jesus and the beloved disciple, at the foot of Jesus's Cross — which is, perhaps, unlikely (at least not without heavy bribery or a serious lapse in security).[20] The important thing about the women's presence, in all four Gospels, is that they were there to bear witness to the reality of Jesus's death — and that some of their number will be the first witnesses to the reality of the resurrection.

---

[15] Mark 15:24, Matthew 27:34f, cf. John 19:23–5a.

[16] See, for example, the apostles' speeches to the Jerusalem crowds (e.g. Acts 3:12–26) and to the authorities (Acts 5:29–32) and Paul's address in Pisidian Antioch (Acts 13:16–41).

[17] Mark 15:40, Matthew 27:55.

[18] Mark 15:41, cf. Luke 8:1b–3.

[19] Mark 16:1.

[20] John 19:25b.

Going against the Crowd

We end our survey of the 'faces in the crowd'—or rather the crowds—around Jesus by considering one man who is going against the crowd. Simon of Cyrene, 'coming in from the country' (Mark 15:21), as everyone else is on their way out of town, is a classic case of the person caught up in events that are nothing to do with him and forced against his will to play a central part.

Simon appears in just one verse in each of the first three Gospels, and neither Matthew nor Luke adds anything to what is recorded by Mark: but from that one verse we are able to deduce quite a lot about him.

First, he was from North Africa. Cyrene was one of the old-established Greek cities on the coast of Libya, founded by settlers from the islands and the Peloponnese six centuries before. It was (and still is) an important centre for trade. There is a famous picture on a Greek cup in the Louvre of one of the early rulers of Cyrene supervising the loading of a ship with bales of cargo. By the time of Jesus most of the people of Cyrene were of mixed Greek and Berber descent. There was also a sizeable Jewish community there, with members sufficiently well-off to travel to Jerusalem for the great festivals, and to provide at least some kind of resident presence in the city.[21]

Simon's name suggests strongly that he belonged to that community, although the name 'Simon' was not exclusively Jewish. It is quite possible that he was a gentile with a snub nose (which is what 'Simon' means in Greek). His two sons, Alexander

---

[21] Acts 2:10.

and Rufus, certainly bear non-Jewish names—but then, so did a couple of Jesus's disciples, and there is no doubt that they were 'kosher'.[22] And at least two Jewish Alexanders are mentioned elsewhere in the New Testament, one of them a member of the high-priestly family.[23]

We also know, from the way in which Mark mentions Simon's sons, that they belonged to (or were known to) the Christian community for which he wrote his Gospel. Their names were, perhaps, put forward by Mark as witnesses to the truth of what he was writing. We know from the Acts of the Apostles that, while some of the Cyrenaic community in Jerusalem were violently opposed to the first followers of Jesus,[24] others had become Christians early on. They were, Luke tells us, among the group in Antioch who were the first to take the initiative of telling non-Jews about Jesus.[25]

All that, of course, is a very long way from Simon, coming in from the country, as Jesus was being led out to execution. The wrong man, as he was to discover, in the wrong place at the wrong time, and going in the wrong direction. He was turned round by the soldiers, loaded with Jesus's Cross and made an honorary member of the execution squad.

Scholars do not know why Simon was press-ganged into carrying the Cross. John's statement that 'Jesus went out carrying the cross by himself' (John 19:17) reflects the usual practice—although, as is often the case, it is likely that John says that for theological reasons rather than in the cause of strict historical accuracy. It was, however, normally part of the punishment for a man sentenced to crucifixion that he had to

---

[22] Andrew and Philip—and possibly the two Simons, although their name as noted in the text is bilingual.

[23] Acts 4:6 and 19:33.

[24] Acts 6:9ff.

[25] Acts 11:20.

carry his own cross-beam (not the whole cross, despite the traditional depiction of this in Christian art down the centuries). The condemned man would bear the cross-beam on his back to the place of execution, where it (and he) would be fastened to the upright, which was a permanent fixture there—probably one of many. There is the ancient tradition of Jesus's three falls, which are part of the traditional 'Stations of the Cross'. Some have suggested that after his rough handling by the Jewish and Roman authorities, culminating in the flogging ordered by Pilate, Jesus was too weak to bear the weight on his own.

The commentator, Ched Myers, points out the ironies in this brief episode.[26] Jesus had entered Jerusalem accompanied willingly by joyful crowds of country people from Galilee and Judaea, waving branches and throwing their cloaks in his path. He leaves it in a Roman procession, accompanied by one press-ganged North African who bears the instrument of a painful and humiliating death rather than an emblem of rejoicing. The name, Simon, too, is not without its ironic overtones. Simon of Cyrene takes up the cross and goes with Jesus, however unwillingly, to the place of death. Simon Peter, who had vowed the night before to go with Jesus to prison and to death, becomes a deserter, denying his Lord three times before cock-crow. Simon of Cyrene, the outsider, becomes the model disciple, responding, albeit unwittingly, to the call to discipleship which Jesus had issued in chapter 8 of Mark's Gospel. Simon Peter (like the rest of the Twelve) is nowhere to be seen.

Christopher Evans, in his commentary on Luke's Gospel, notes at this point that the picture of Simon of Cyrene as the 'model disciple' is flawed, because Simon is compelled, while disciples (ideally) act of their own free will when they answer the call to 'deny themselves and take up their cross and follow'

---

[26] Myers, *Binding the Strong Man*, 385.

(Mark 8:34).[27] But I am not sure how far that is a valid point. It is by no means unknown for Christians to find their discipleship deepened, or their initial call occurring, in situations where they cannot exercise free will, bereavement, perhaps, or some other major life crisis. How many people have come to a deeper Christian commitment because other doors have been shut and there is no other way out that they can take with integrity? How many people have found, in James Montgomery's words:

> Patience to watch, and wait, and weep,
> Though mercy long delay,
> Courage our fainting souls to keep,
> And trust thee though thou slay.[28]

—in circumstances where, like Simon of Cyrene, they had, in truth, no realistic alternative?

So today, as we look at the last of our 'Faces in the Crowd', we recognize, perhaps, our own face in the face of this frustrated, angry, frightened man, forced to turn aside from his chosen path, compelled to take his place in humiliation alongside a man on his way to a shameful, agonizing death. And we recognize the power of that condemned man, mocked, tortured, abandoned by his friends, to challenge and to transform those whose lives touch his, in whatever circumstances. We recognize his death as the point from which life truly begins. We begin to grasp that it is the way down, death followed by resurrection, life through dying, which is the way up. That is part of what it means to be human. It is not confined to a single event (Christ's death and resurrection), nor does it apply only in the closing stages of life. It is central to our human existence. Repeatedly in the Gospels Jesus warns those who follow him, or who want to

---

[27] Christopher F. Evans, *St Luke*, TPI New Testament Commentaries (SCM Press, 1990), 860–1.

[28] NEH 406.

follow him, that if they seek to hang on to what they have of life, they are lost.[29] It is those who are prepared to let go and do the necessary dying, who will receive a fuller, richer quality of life.

To quote Bishop John V. Taylor again, this time from the last of the Holy Week addresses which he gave in Geneva in 1985:

> In any lifetime there are innumerable little deaths — always painful and frightening — changing house, seeing a child go away from home for the first time, losing one's job, leaving one's homeland, the break-up of a marriage, retirement — you can think of many more. There are also for every woman and man occasions when a dying for others is required — one's own cherished plan surrendered so that someone else may have a more important breakthrough; one's work used and the credit given to someone who may need it more; one's lifestyle curtailed by another's demand upon us; one's security sacrificed so that others may be helped. It hardly ever happens with any heroics or romance. It is hard and unacknowledged … And how may we visualise … until it breaks upon us.[30]

---

[29] A form of this saying appears in all four Gospels (Matt. 10:39, Mark 8:35, Luke 9:24, John 12:25). Matthew and Luke regard it as so important that they repeat it, at 16:25 and 17:33, respectively.

[30] Taylor, *Weep Not for Me*, 42f.

Epilogue
The Roman Governor

When Pilate heard these words, he brought Jesus outside and sat on the judge's bench at a place called The Stone Pavement, or in Hebrew Gabbatha. Now it was the day of Preparation for the Passover; and it was about noon. He said to the Jews, 'Here is your King!' They cried out, 'Away with him! Away with him! Crucify him!' Pilate asked them, 'Shall I crucify your King?' The chief priests answered, 'We have no king but the emperor.' Then he handed him over to them to be crucified. (John 19:13–16a)

Our final interlude takes us a few hundred yards to the north-west. It is no great distance from the house of the High Priest to the palace of King Herod, butting up against the western wall of the city. Not that the royal family had a great deal of use of it these days. The Roman governor tended to stay there, in preference to the grim fortress of Antonia, his official residence, when he was in Jerusalem on important business, as he usually was for the duration of major festivals, and as he always was for Passover week. By comparison with some recent Passovers, this has been one of the less eventful festivals. There have been no major disturbances to public order. And so, this year, on the night of the Passover Sabbath, the members of the governor's staff are relaxing. However, a light is still burning in the governor's private quarters. The procurator himself is not yet able to relax. He is pacing up and down the room, pausing for thought from time to time, as he dictates the following report to his private secretary:

From Pontius Pilate, Procurator of the Province of Judaea

To Tiberius Caesar Augustus, son of the deified Augustus, grandson of the deified Julius (and all the other honours and titles which are currently approved for use in official dispatches), greeting.

I am writing this report on the day after the Jewish feast of Passover, and it is with pleasure and satisfaction that I can report to Caesar a quiet Passover season in Judea this year. Those who have first-hand knowledge of the Jewish people and their outlandish customs will be aware that this is the season when Jews remember the time when their God is supposed to have freed them from slavery to a foreign power and brought them to settle in this land. It is therefore a season when relations between the Jews and representatives of Roman authority are even more than usually sensitive, particularly here in Jerusalem, their holy city. In previous years I have had to report more than once on the robust response of our forces to an upsurge of nationalist agitation and violent demonstrations against the power of Rome.

This year, I am happy to report that no such severe measures were necessary. Military force in Jerusalem was kept to the bare minimum required to maintain the honour and dignity of the Governor. Nor was it necessary to authorize covert operations against terrorists or other subversive groups.

It was however necessary for me to take resolute action on one occasion towards the end of the festival in order to prevent a situation from getting out of hand and blowing up into a full-scale crisis. The source of the trouble was one of the Jews' so-called holy men, a wandering Galilean preacher who has something of a reputation in this province as a healer and exorcist. He has been kept under surveillance in the past but intelligence reports reaching me did not suggest that he posed any serious danger to the interests of Rome. In some respects he has been, if anything, positive towards the army of occupation, encouraging his followers not to refuse the legitimate demands of our troops and rejecting an invitation to incite non-payment of taxes. Indeed, he has (unlike many religious leaders in Palestine) welcomed among his followers people who have collaborated with Roman power. The man's name is Jesus. He is a carpenter by trade and comes from the village of Nazareth, which lies within the Galilean jurisdiction of Prince Herod.

Caesar may rest assured that I have taken care to see that the Prince has been kept fully informed at all stages of our investigations. In preparation for the formal trial before my tribunal, the man Jesus was in fact referred to him for interrogation on matters relating to his activities in Galilee.

Jesus of Nazareth was arrested by the Temple Police and transferred to me for trial and sentence after a preliminary hearing before the appropriate Jewish authorities. This represents a gratifying change in their position. The Jews have tended to be extremely touchy about any action on our part which might be interpreted as infringing what they regard as their 'rights' under the terms of our occupation. Willing co-operation of this kind shows how much progress has been made since the various unfortunate misunderstandings which occurred earlier in my term of office as governor.

However, this is not to say that the case of Jesus of Nazareth was straightforward. Far from it. Initially I was uncertain how far it was proper for me to be involved.

In this country religious and political matters are so closely intertwined that it is sometimes difficult to distinguish one from the other. Speaking for myself, I have always considered that the gods are to be paid the honour due to them in order to ensure the safety and security of Caesar and of the Senate and People of Rome. However, neither I nor my staff can pretend to understand why the more educated Jews argue with such seriousness (not to say ferocity) over the smallest matters relating to their God and to the code of law which they claim he handed down to them in a distant past—earlier even than the foundation of Rome.

My initial inclination, given the demeanour of the prisoner and the intelligence reports on his activities, was to release him, after administering minor chastisement in the shape of a flogging, partly as a gesture to the Jewish authorities (who were out in force to support the charges against him) and partly as a token of my displeasure at the inconvenience and waste of government time. However, in the course of questioning it became apparent that the case raised issues of importance for the security of the province. There was a religious status allegedly claimed by the prisoner which might also be construed as a claim to some kind of kingship. When pressed on this the prisoner gave evasive answers and from time to time he would retreat into long periods of silence.

At this stage I had no firm evidence on which to base the death sentence that was being demanded by the Jewish authorities and the crowd which (notwithstanding the early hour) had accompanied them to Government House. Intelligence reports, as I have said, were not unfavourable. Nor, despite his evasions and silences, did the prisoner give me any serious reason to doubt their essential accuracy.

I attempted to convey this to the Jewish leaders and their supporters. The intensity of their reaction and the depth of their hostility to the prisoner took me (I must confess) by surprise. It is, to say the least, unusual for a Roman magistrate to be urging clemency in such a case, and neither I nor my subordinates have a reputation for softness in our dealings with the native population, as Caesar will be well aware.

At one stage I attempted to win them round by offering freedom for a prisoner as a mark of respect for the festival. I regret that this manoeuvre was less than totally successful. The prisoner on whose release the crowd insisted was not Jesus of Nazareth, as I had hoped, but a notorious nationalist agitator and terrorist. However, this man's associates are well known to us and I have every confidence that he will be returned to custody very swiftly.

I must add that by this stage the mood of the crowd was increasingly ugly and it was clear that, unless decisive action was taken by me to regain control of the situation, a serious disturbance of the peace was likely to ensue. Caesar will, no doubt, recollect that in a previous report I outlined the extreme difficulty of using armed military force to over-awe the people of Jerusalem in any matter where their religion is concerned. In anything that reflects on the honour and worship of their God, Jews will suffer indignity, torture and even death rather than compromise their beliefs. It is this which makes Judaea a particularly difficult province to govern effectively.

Short of ordering the Jerusalem garrison and my own bodyguard into the crowd with drawn swords, I had few options open to me. I therefore took the difficult decision to condemn Jesus of Nazareth to the extreme punishment. The sentence of crucifixion was duly carried out by a detachment of our troops later that day, 25 March, at the execution ground known locally as 'Skull Hill' which lies to the north-west side of the city.

In the charge-sheet affixed to the gallows, it was made clear to all the considerable crowd of spectators that the prisoner was condemned as a political criminal and not because of any offence against Jewish law. That would not have been a matter for Rome's concern. This message was reinforced by crucifying him with two known nationalist agents, associates of the man whom I had released. I cannot say that their reported conduct towards their companion in misery either reinforced or removed any doubts about the correctness of the sentence.

I trust that the contents of this report will be sufficient to counter any accusations of disloyalty to Caesar which may have reached Rome from hostile sources in Jerusalem. I have always sought strenuously to deserve the title of 'Caesar's friend' which was so graciously awarded on my appointment to Judaea, by upholding the dignity of Caesar and the interests of the Senate and People of Rome to the best of my ability. Caesar may rest assured that I will continue to do so for as long as I hold office.

Which brings me to my final point: the governorship of Judaea is a sensitive and demanding post even in peaceful times. I have served Caesar as Procurator of this province for a number of years now, in difficult times. It is not an easy posting—the need to divide my time between the Governor's residence in Caesarea and the Antonia fortress in Jerusalem is a considerable drain on time and energy. Furthermore because of the nature of the country and the people, the usual compensations of a provincial governorship are not easily to be found. One consequence of the difficulties that we have experienced during these years has been a marked deterioration in my wife's state of health. These past days have been particularly stressful for us both and I am anxious that she may be in danger of suffering a complete breakdown. I would therefore humbly request Caesar to consider my application for transfer to an alternative posting (or even early relief and retirement) as a matter of some urgency.

Bibliography

Christophe F. Evans, *St Luke*, TPI New Testament Commentaries (SCM Press, 1990).

Martin Hengel, *The Cross of the Son of God*, trans. John Bowden (SCM Press, 1976).

Joachim Jeremias, *Jerusalem in the Time of Jesus: An Investigation into Economic and Social Conditions during the New Testament Period*, trans. F. H. and C. H. Cave (Fortress Press, 1969).

Flavius Josephus, *The Jewish War*, trans. G. A. Williamson (Penguin Classics, 1959).

Ched Myers, *Binding the Strong Man: A Political Reading of Mark's Story of Jesus* (Orbis, 1988).

Hermann Samuel Reimarus, *The Goal of Jesus and his Disciples*, trans. and introd. George Wesley Buchanan (Brill, 1970).

Albert Schweitzer, *The Quest of the Historical Jesus: A Critical Study of its Progress from Reimarus to Wrede*, trans. William Montgomery (A. and C. Black, 1910).

John V. Taylor, *Weep Not for Me: Meditations on the Cross and the Resurrection* (World Council of Churches, 1986).

Gerd Theissen, *The Shadow of the Galilean*, trans. John Bowden (Fortress Press, 1987).

Cornelius Tacitus, *The Histories*, trans. Kenneth Wellesley (Penguin Classics, 1964).

———, *The Annals*, trans. Michael Grant (Penguin Classics, 1958).

SLG PRESS PUBLICATIONS

FP1 *Prayer and the Life of Reconciliation* — Gilbert Shaw (1969)

FP2 *Aloneness not Loneliness* — Mother Mary Clare SLG (1969)

FP4 *Intercession* — Mother Mary Clare SLG (1969)

FP8 *Prayer: Extracts from the Teaching of Father Gilbert Shaw* — Gilbert Shaw (1973)

FP12 *Learning to Pray* — Mother Mary Clare SLG (1970, rev. 3/2025)

FP15 *Death, the Gateway to Life* — Gilbert Shaw (1971, 3/2024)

FP16 *The Victory of the Cross* — Dumitru Stăniloae (1970, 3/2023)

FP26 *The Message of Saint Seraphim* — Irina Gorainov (1974)

FP28 *Julian of Norwich: Four Studies to Commemorate the Sixth Centenary of the Revelations of Divine Love* — Sister Benedicta Ward SLG, Sister Eileen Mary SLG, Sister Mary Paul SLG, A. M. Allchin (1973, 3/2022)

FP43 *The Power of the Name: The Jesus Prayer in Orthodox Spirituality* — Kallistos Ware (1974)

FP46 *Prayer and Contemplation* and *Distractions are for Healing* — Robert Llewelyn (1975, rev. 4/2025)

FP48 *The Wisdom of the Desert Fathers* — trans. Sister Benedicta Ward SLG (1975)

FP50 *Letters of Saint Antony the Great* — trans. Derwas Chitty (1975, 2/2021)

FP54 *From Loneliness to Solitude* — Roland Walls (1976)

FP55 *Theology and Spirituality* — Andrew Louth (1976, rev. 1978, 3/2024)

FP61 *Kabir: The Way of Love and Paradox* — Sister Rosemary SLG (1977)

FP62 *Anselm of Canterbury: A Monastic Scholar* — Sister Benedicta Ward SLG (1973, 2/2024)

FP67 *Mary and the Mystery of the Incarnation: An Essay on the Mother of God in the Theology of Karl Barth* — Andrew Louth (1977, 2/2024)

FP68 *Trinity and Incarnation in Anglican Tradition* — A. M. Allchin (1977, rev. 2/2025)

FP70 *Facing Depression* — Gonville ffrench-Beytagh (1978, 2/2020)

FP71 *The Single Person* — Philip Welsh (1979)

FP72 *The Letters of Ammonas, Successor of St Antony* — trans. Derwas Chitty, introd. Sebastian Brock (1979, 2/2023)

FP74 *George Herbert, Priest and Poet* — Kenneth Mason (1980)

FP75 *A Study of Wisdom: Three Tracts by the Author of The Cloud of Unknowing* — trans. Clifton Wolters (1980)

FP81 *The Psalms: Prayer Book of the Bible* — Dietrich Bonhoeffer, trans. Sister Isabel SLG (1982, rev. 3/2025)

FP82 *Prayer & Holiness: The Icon of Man Renewed in God* — Dumitru Stăniloae (1982, rev. 2/2023)

FP85 *Walter Hilton: Eight Chapters on Perfection & Angels' Song* — trans. Rosemary Dorward (1983, rev. 3/2024)

FP88 *Creative Suffering* — Iulia de Beausobre (1989)

FP90 *Bringing Forth Christ: Five Feasts of the Child Jesus by St Bonaventure* — trans. Eric Doyle OFM (1984, 3/2024)

FP92 *Gentleness in John of the Cross* — Thomas Kane (1985, rev. 2/2025)

FP94 *Saint Gregory Nazianzen: Selected Poems* — trans. John McGuckin (1986, 2/2024)

FP95 *The World of the Desert Fathers: Stories and Sayings from the Anonymous Series of the Apophthegmata Patrum* — trans. Columba Stewart OSB (1986, 2/2020)

FP104 *Growing Old with God* — Timothy N. Rudd (1988, 2/2020)

FP106 *Julian Reconsidered* — Kenneth Leech, Sister Benedicta Ward SLG (1988, rev. 2/2024)

FP108 *The Unicorn: Meditations on the Love of God* — Harry Galbraith Miller (1989)

www.slgpress.co.uk

The Sisters of the Love of God is an Anglican community of women religious living a contemplative monastic life.

To learn more about the Community and the Convent of the Incarnation at Fairacres, Oxford, see our website www.slg.org.uk.

As well as supporting those seeking to follow a vocation to the monastic life, the Community has a number of forms of association for those who feel drawn to share in the Sisters' life of prayer: Fellowship of the Love of God, Companions, Priests Associate and Oblate Sisters.

For more information email sisters@slg.org.uk or write to The Reverend Mother, Convent of the Incarnation, Parker Street, Oxford, OX4 1TB, UK.